Growing as a follower of Jesus

Exploring the New Testament to discover how people follow Jesus

This book belongs to ....

I am ....(Age)

People sometimes call me ....(My Nickname)

I live at ....

....

For Parents

One of the amazing things about the Bible is that every time you read it, you can get something more and something different out of it.

The writers of this book believe that the Bible isn't just an interesting history book. In a mysterious way, God uses the Bible to help us to learn about God and about how to live on earth today, even though our world is completely different from the world of either the Old or New Testaments.

But because our world *is* so different, and because the Bible can be hard to understand sometimes, we need help – help in explaining the contexts in which certain books were written, and help in understanding what about the Bible is relevant for us today.

This book, part of the ***Hotshots*** series, looks at the question of what living as a follower of Jesus might mean. It starts with the Sermon on the Mount, where Jesus talks about being his follower and how this might shape our lives and the way we act.

It then goes on to look at various people who did choose to become Jesus' disciples, as well as some who didn't. Some of these stories are told in the Gospels and others in the book of Acts, which tells of the adventures of the early Christians, after Jesus had left the earth.

We hope that as children read this little book the stories of the early followers of Jesus will grab their attention. And we hope that this will in turn lead them to think about what being a follower of Jesus might mean in their own lives.

Getting Started with Hotshots

The Bible is a large book. Where do you begin?

Find out how the Hotshots go about it.

You can choose when and where to do your reading.

I always do my Hotshots when I get home from school. I write important things in a scrapbook.

What you will need:

- A pen
- Scissors
- Coloured pencils or pens

I like to read my Hotshots book each morning before I go to school. If I need to remember anything I will make a message on my cassette recorder.

I like to read my Hotshots before I go to bed. I usually put my ideas on my computer.

What about you?

On the clock, draw what time is best for you.

Write here where you will read your Hotshots book

_____

Meet the HOTSHOTS

They're incredible!

The Hotshots meet every Friday evening. They like to have fun and to practise basketball. They also have something to eat. They like pizza and coke best. Sometimes they watch a video or tell some jokes. They make sure they warm up properly before playing. And they enjoy finding out about the Bible. Jeff, their leader and coach helps them with that. He seems to know everything about God and the Bible. And when they play, every now and then the team wins a basketball match, but not very often!

Put yourself in the picture! Draw yourself in this team photo.

Kim Dan Anna Samuel Chris Hong Emily Jeff

How to find your way in the Bible

You will soon find that the Bible sections you need are printed in this Hotshots book. These Bible bits come from many parts of the New Testament.

The Bible has chapters and verses to help you find your place. It's like an address but its called a reference.

| The book of the Bible | The chapter (Chapter 5) | The verses (Verses 1 and 2) |

Matthew 5:1-2

If you want to find the place in your own Bible first look up the Contents page near the start of the Bible. You will find that Matthew is found at the beginning of the New Testament.

Try this fun test. Look up this verse and answer the questions.

Matthew 4:18

What beach was Jesus walking along?

☐ ☐ ☐ ☐ ☐ ☐ ☐

Who were the two brothers he invited to join him?

☐ ☐ ☐ ☐ ☐

and ☐ ☐ ☐ ☐ ☐ ☐

Now you're ready to go!

Welcome to Hotshots!

Teacher and friend

It was the last 'time-out' of the match. The team gathered around Jeff listening for any instructions for the rest of the game.

Matthew 5:1-3

[1] When Jesus saw the crowds, he went up on the side of a mountain and sat down.

Jesus' disciples gathered around him, [2] and he taught them:

[3] "God blesses those people who depend only on him. They belong to the kingdom of heaven!"

On the next page, draw the disciples sitting around Jesus, eagerly listening to him.

If you like you can draw yourself in the picture too!

The disciples were already followers of Jesus. Now he is teaching them more important things about the way to live.

Prayer: *Thank you Jesus that you are teacher and friend for so many people, even today.*

Draw the disciples sitting around Jesus.

Happy people

Matthew 5:4-6

4 "God blesses those people who grieve. They will find comfort!

5 God blesses those people who are humble. The earth will belong to them!

6 God blesses those people who want to obey him more than to eat or drink. They will be given what they want!"

Verse 6 reminds us of the best choice we can ever make. Blessing or help is specially for people who truly want to obey God in their lives.

Prayer: *Lord Jesus, please help me to choose your way.*

Magic letters

Fill in the missing magic letters – the vowels a,e,i,o,u.

God blesses those people who want to obey him…

m__r__ th__n t__ __ __t __r dr__nk. *(That's a lot!)*

Life is full of choices. Just because "everyone does it" doesn't mean they are right.

Some of the kids at school say I'm mad to train so often. While I'm working hard, they are watching TV or playing computer games or lazing around.

3 Inside out

Matthew 5:7-8

7 "God blesses those people who are merciful. They will be treated with mercy!
8 God blesses those people whose hearts are pure. They will see him!"

Jesus reminds us that the kind of person we are on the *inside* is more important than how we look on the *outside*.

What kind of thing might Hong say back to Chris?
(*Tick your choice*)

☐ What's the weather like up there?

☐ It's what you're really like inside that counts

☐ Just wait, I might end up bigger than you!

☐ Don't be so bossy

Sometimes it's hard to be kind (merciful) to people who hurt us.

We need Jesus to help us live his way.

Prayer: *Dear Lord Jesus, please help me today to be the same on both the inside and the outside.*

Something good to make!

Anna had noticed Chris making fun of Hong. She had not heard what Chris said, but could tell what was happening from the look on their faces and Chris' actions.

What should she do?

☐ Help Hong to think of a way to get even with Chris?

☐ Tell others of the team and try to get them on Hong's side?

☐ Try to make peace between the boys?

Matthew 5:9-10

[9] "God blesses those people who make peace. They will be called his children!

[10] God blesses those people who are treated badly for doing right. They belong to the kingdom of heaven."

Find the pencil or pen of your favourite colour and underline the verse that shows Anna what she should do (verse 9).

Prayer: *Lord Jesus, please help me be a peacemaker even when it's hard.*

Popular people

Who are the most popular kids in your class? _____

Why do you think this is so?

WOW!
Imagine winning the gold trophy for "Most Popular Player" at BB Association Awards Night.

☐   Because they are good at sports?

☐   Because they are good looking?

☐   Because they seem to have lots of things?

☐   Some other reason? _____

Is being popular important?

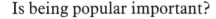
Matthew 5:11-12

11 "God will bless you when people insult you, mistreat you, and tell all kinds of evil lies about you because of me.
12 Be happy and excited! You will have a great reward in heaven. People did these same things to the prophets who lived long ago."

What a hard life! Jesus had to put up with hurtful and unkind words from people who didn't believe in him. This can happen to his followers today also.

Jesus says even if people tease or laugh at you because you believe in him, be happy. You are on the winning side.

Prayer: *Lord Jesus help me remember that following your way is more important than being popular.*

Being angry

Today is Hotshots Church Parade. They must all wear their team tracksuits to the service.

Matthew 5:21-24

[21] You know that our ancestors were told, "Do not murder" and "A murderer must be brought to trial." [22] But I promise you that if you are angry with someone, you will have to stand trial. If you call someone a fool, you will be taken to court. And if you say that someone is worthless, you will be in danger of the fires of hell.

[23] So if you are about to place your gift on the altar and remember that someone is angry with you, [24] leave your gift there in front of the altar. Make peace with that person, then come back and offer your gift to God.

As Kim changed into her old tracksuit she remembered what Jesus said about being angry. She was *ready* for church but she was *not truly ready*. Not until she'd made peace with her little sister.

Prayer:
Thank you for all the good and helpful things in the Bible. Help me put them into practice.

When anger explodes like a storm

When someone is angry with you...
1. Be calm
2. Be polite
3. Be forgiving

You will be feeling hurt and disappointed but this will pass. Try not to let your hurt grow and get worse. If you have the chance, try to tell the person how you feel and look for a way to be friends again.

When you feel angry with someone ...
Remember, it happens to everyone.
And it happens before you can think about it.
1. Count to 10 and try to relax!
2. Try to explain why you are angry.
3. Think of a way to solve your problem by talking about it. Try not to keep your anger locked inside.

Tell God how you feel. Remember, God knows about it already!

Making promises

Matthew 5:33-37

33 You know that our ancestors were told, "Don't use the Lord's name to make a promise unless you are going to keep it." 34 But I tell you not to swear by anything when you make a promise! Heaven is God's throne, so don't swear by heaven. 35 The earth is God's footstool, so don't swear by the earth. Jerusalem is the city of the great king, so don't swear by it. 36 Don't swear by your own head. You cannot make one hair white or black. 37 When you make a promise, say only "Yes" or "No."

Jesus tells us that we should keep our promises. Then there will be no need to swear at all. Everyone will know that we are trustworthy.

When we're making a promise Jesus says *two* words are all we need.

Write them in these boxes.

☐   or   ☐

Prayer: *Help me please Lord Jesus to be always trustworthy and honest. Help me to keep my promises.*

8 Revenge

Many, many years ago, teachers and leaders made a law to make sure people were treated fairly. The law said it was fair to pay back so long as you took only what was taken from you – no more. This law tried to stop people from making things worse.

Matthew 5:38-42

38 You know that you have been taught, "An eye for an eye and a tooth for a tooth." 39 But I tell you not to try to get even with a person who has done something to you. When someone slaps your right cheek, turn and let that person slap your other cheek. 40 If someone sues you for your shirt, give up your coat as well. 41 If a soldier forces you to carry his pack one kilometre, carry it two kilometres. 42 When people ask you for something, give it to them. When they want to borrow money, lend it to them.

So it was Anna who hid my shoe and made me late. I'll get her for that!

It must have been Anna who hid my shoe. Now I am late. It's probably a joke. It'll be OK.

This law seemed good and fair, but Jesus had a better way. He wanted to change things for ever! He banned paying people back altogether. It's better not to keep fighting and hurting each other.

Tick the picture above which is most like what Jesus taught.

Prayer: *Following Jesus takes courage. Ask him to help you.*

Don't pay back... show love

9 Love

Jesus keeps surprising people with his ideas about a new way to live.

Matthew 5:43-48

43 You have heard people say, "Love your neighbours and hate your enemies." 44 But I tell you to love your enemies and pray for anyone who mistreats you. 45 Then you will be acting like your Father in heaven. He makes the sun rise on both good and bad people. And he sends rain for the ones who do right and for the ones who do wrong. 46 If you love only those people who love you, will God reward you for that? Even tax collectors love their friends. 47 If you greet only your friends, what's so great about that? Don't even unbelievers do that? 48 But you must always act like your Father in heaven.

Love *continued ...*

1. What to do to people you don't like. (*Tick one*)

   ☐ Hate them

   ☐ Ignore them

   ☐ Love them

   ☐ Refuse to speak to them

2. What to do to people who are unkind to you. (*Tick one*)

   ☐ Hate them

   ☐ Pray for them

   ☐ Don't play with them

   ☐ Refuse to speak to them

Think and pray:

Do you know someone you really don't like? Say a prayer now especially for that person:

Lord Jesus, I find it hard to like

_____.

Please help me today to do something kind for them.

Let's copy Jesus' great example.

10 Showing off about money

I've raised $19.65. I bet that's more than anyone else has.

Sam and Dan decided to raise some money for a children's charity.

Dan had raised $25, but he didn't say anything.
Read the Bible passage below and see if you can work out why.

Read Matthew 6:1-4

[1] When you do good deeds, don't try to show off. If you do, you won't get a reward from your Father in heaven.

[2] When you give to the poor, don't blow your own trumpet. That's what show-offs do in the meeting places and on the street corners, because they are always looking for praise. I can assure you that they already have their reward.

[3] When you give to the poor, don't let anyone know about it. [4] Then your gift will be given in secret. Your Father knows what's done in secret, and he will reward you.

Why did Dan keep quiet?

_____

_____

Prayer: Lord, please help me not to boast when I help someone. You already know what I've done and that's the most important thing.

Use a mirror to try reading this message.

Jesus says,
'Don't boast about the
good things you do.'

Showing off about praying

Who do you know who is a show-off? Do they annoy you? Why?

Matthew 6:5-7

[5] When you pray, don't be like those show-offs who love to stand up and pray in the meeting places and on the street corners. They do this just to look good. I can assure you that they already have their reward.

[6] When you pray, go into a room alone and close the door. Pray to your Father in private, and he will reward you.

[7] When you pray, don't talk on and on as people do who don't know God. They think God likes to hear long prayers. [8] Don't be like them. Your Father knows what you need before you ask.

God you're very special! WOW!!

Some people show off when giving money to needy people. Others show off when they pray. You may think you are all alone in your bedroom – or even outdoors –when you say a simple prayer like Emily. But remember, something wonderful is happening.

If you're honest in what you're saying, the God of all the Universe is listening to you and loving you. Our God is much, much greater than anyone else you can ever think of – WOW! Isn't that wonderful!

Think and pray:
Spend some time now, quietly thinking about this. Then pray.

The Lord's Prayer

Matthew 6:9-15

[9] You should pray like this:

Our Father in heaven, help us to honour your name.

[10] Come and set up your kingdom, so that everyone on earth will obey you, as you are obeyed in heaven.

[11] Give us our food for today.

[12] Forgive us for doing wrong, as we forgive others.

[13] Keep us from being tempted and protect us from evil.

[14] If you forgive others for the wrongs they do to you, your Father in heaven will forgive you. [15] But if you don't forgive others, your Father will not forgive your sins.

With your favourite felt pens or colour pencils, decorate the frame to show how important this prayer is.

Jesus teaches us about praying

The Lord's Prayer is very well known. You probably pray it in your church or Kid's Club.

These verses are the beginning of a 'pattern prayer' which Jesus taught us. For today we will just think about verses 9 and 10.

Think: *Imagine our world if verse 10 had already happened. Spend some time thinking about what it would be like.*

Maybe the 'pattern prayer' that Jesus taught will help us to learn to pray.

Forgiving is the best way

Today we will think again about Jesus' 'pattern prayer'. Look again at the prayer on page 20 and think especially about verses 11 to 15.

There are 3 things we are asking from God in this part of the prayer. Cross out the wrong one.

1. Please forgive us for the wrong things we do.

2. Please give us lots of things.

3. Please help us not to do wrong things.

4. Please give us what we really need today.

I'll never forgive Emily for that sloppy pass. It's *her* fault I lost the ball.

I think you should forgive her mistake.

She really feels bad about it you know. *She'll* feel better and *you'll* feel better if you forgive.

Prayer: Use Jesus' 'pattern prayer' to make your own prayer today.

Time out with God

In basketball, time out is a time to listen to the coach to make sure that you have understood their instructions. Everyone needs time out with God. It is a way to make sure that you have the chance to talk to him about anything that is on your mind – maybe something that is bothering you.

Five important things to remember:

1. You can talk with God at any time. You can be alone or with friends.

2. You can talk with God about anything. Sad things, happy things, things that worry you, things you are thankful about, things that have made you feel disappointed. You can talk to him about other people – your family, your friends, people who are sick or in trouble, people who work for others.

3. You can talk to God anywhere. You don't need to be in a church. You can have time out with God just where you are.

4. You don't have to invent a special language. He knows what you are thinking about even when you don't tell him.

5. You can whisper if you like, or talk aloud or even think the things you want to say in your head. He can even 'hear' that kind of praying.

continued overpage

It is a great idea to make sure you have some time out with God each day. Perhaps this can be just after you read your Hotshots book.

To help you with this time out with God, here is a list of ideas for things to pray about. This list is already printed in the Hotshots book *The world's greatest leader – ever!*

Sunday: Pray for your church and the people who lead it

Monday: Pray for your teacher and friends at school

Tuesday: Pray for members of your family

Wednesday: Pray for things that you need help with

Thursday: Pray about people who are really ill

Friday: Pray about the sad things in the world that you see on TV

Saturday: Pray for your best friends

14 People and things

What things are bothering you today?

The girls in my new school are not very friendly. If I had better clothes and lots of pocket-money, they would want to become my friends.

Matthew 6:25-26

25 I tell you not to worry about your life. Don't worry about having something to eat, drink, or wear. Isn't life more than food or clothing? 26 Look at the birds in the sky! They don't plant or harvest. They don't even store grain in barns. Yet your Father in heaven takes care of them. Aren't you worth more than birds?

Jesus was *not* saying, 'You must never think about these things at all.'

Jesus *was* saying, 'Remember, there are more important things.'

Dear Kim

Read once again what Jesus said, then write down here the advice you would give Kim.

Prayer: *Thank you Heavenly Father that you take good care of me.*

Learning from your garden

Next time you're outside, check out what colours, shapes and perfumes you can find in the various plants. They are all part of God's wonderful creation.

You are an even *more precious* part of his creation. He cares about *you*.

Matthew 6:27-30

27 Can worry make you live longer? 28 Why worry about clothes? Look how the wild flowers grow. They don't work hard to make their clothes. 29 But I tell you that Solomon with all his wealth wasn't as well clothed as one of them. 30 God gives such beauty to everything that grows in the fields, even though it is here today and thrown into a fire tomorrow. He will surely do even more for you! Why do you have such little faith?

Something to do:

Don't Worry – trust God

Find a piece of plain card and write these words on it. Pick some small flowers and place them on a tissue.

Fold them carefully in the tissue, then place the tissue inside a thick book. Add more heavy books on top. After the flowers dry out (this will take several weeks) stick them onto the card.

Add some ribbon or string. Then hang the card where you will see it often, to remind you of its message.

16 Worry

What sorts of things make you anxious?

Matthew 6:31-34

31 Don't worry and ask yourselves, "Will we have anything to eat? Will we have anything to drink? Will we have any clothes to wear?" 32 Only people who don't know God are always worrying about such things. Your Father in heaven knows that you need all of these. 33 But more than anything else, put God's work first and do what he wants. Then the other things will be yours as well.

34 Don't worry about tomorrow. It will take care of itself. You have enough to worry about today.

Question: How can you stop worrying about things?

Answer: By making God the Number One person in your life.

Think and pray:

Is anything worrying you? Is it really important? Talk to God about it. (You might like to talk to your parents or an older friend about it also.)

Follow the lines and see what Jesus says.

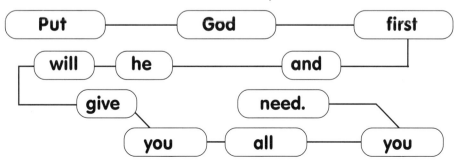

17 Specks and logs

Sometimes Jesus told funny stories so that people would remember the important truth he was teaching.

Matthew 7:1-5

[1] Don't condemn others, and God won't condemn you. [2] God will be as hard on you as you are on others! He will treat you exactly as you treat them.

[3] You can see the speck in your friend's eye, but you don't notice the log in your own eye. [4] How can you say, "My friend, let me take the speck out of your eye," when you don't see the log in your own eye? [5] You're nothing but show-offs! First, take the log out of your own eye. Then you can see how to take the speck out of your friend's eye.

Think: *Ask yourself, 'Are there any logs in my eye?'*

Chris and the Speck

Chris is sticking up for his sister. He feels good.

He wouldn't treat anyone like that.

Chris' Log

Chris is with his mates at school. A new boy comes up. No one ever plays with him.

Good things

Once again, Jesus told a joke to help people remember something important.

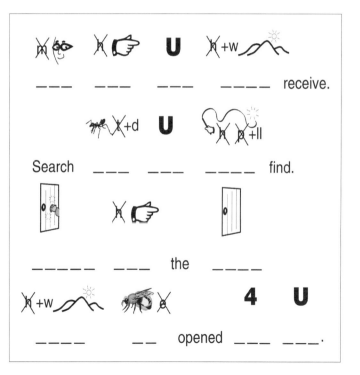

receive.

Search ___ ___ _____ find.

_____ ___ the ____

_____ __ opened ___ ___.

Matthew 7:7-11

[7] Ask, and you will receive. Search, and you will find. Knock, and the door will be opened for you. [8] Everyone who asks will receive. Everyone who searches will find. And the door will be opened for everyone who knocks. [9] Would any of you give your hungry child a stone, if the child asked for some bread? [10] Would you give your child a snake if the child asked for a fish? [11] As bad as you are, you still know how to give good gifts to your children. But your heavenly Father is even more ready to give good things to people who ask.

Most parents look after their children as well as they can. Sometimes, they go without things so that their children will have what they need.

Jesus said, 'God is your father ... even better than the best father on earth. This father knows your needs very well.'

Why not *Say a prayer of thanks to God.*
Thank your parents for all they do for you.

19 Gold!

The Hotshots were in front. With five minutes left on the clock, Emily took a great pass but hurt her finger slightly. From then on, she fumbled. This often resulted in a turnover. The Hotshots lost by 3. They were disappointed.

Matthew 7:12

12 Treat others as you want them to treat you. This is what the Law and the Prophets are all about.

When you don't know how you should be behaving towards someone, stop for a moment. Think how *you* would like that person to behave towards *you*.

This message is so important that it's called *The Golden Rule*.

Survey:

Think of 5-10 adults in your family or street. Ask each of them if they know what 'The Golden Rule' is. Count how many can answer your question. What was your score? _____

Prayer:
I need your help dear God to put this rule into practice.

It's Emily's fault that we lost. I'm going to tell her. It's not fair!

I guess it was because her finger was sore. I'd feel awful if it were me... Poor Emily... I'll go and see how she's feeling.

Choosing

Everyone has to make choices. Some choices are better than others. Jesus asks us to think hard before we make up our minds what is the best, rather than the easiest thing to do.

Matthew 7:13-14

[13] Go in through the narrow gate. The gate to destruction is wide, and the road that leads there is easy to follow. A lot of people go through that gate. [14] But the gate to life is very narrow. The road that leads there is so hard to follow that only a few people find it.

To think and pray about:
Which way are you going? Ask God to help you think about it

Answer TRUE or FALSE
to each of the following sentences.

1. Finding the Jesus way is easy ....

2. Living the Jesus way can be hard..............................

3. Jesus' way leads to life ....

4. The wide, easy road leads to joy ....

The answers are on page 34.

There is more about how to go Jesus' way on page 95.

21

How to tell if it's true

Sometimes friends tell you things that seem too good to be true. It's hard to tell if they are telling the truth.

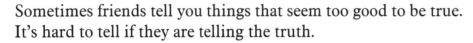

Matthew 7:15-20

¹⁵ Watch out for false prophets! They dress up like sheep, but inside they are wolves who have come to attack you. ¹⁶ You can tell what they are by what they do. No one picks grapes or figs from thorn bushes. ¹⁷ A good tree produces good fruit, and a bad tree produces bad fruit. ¹⁸ A good tree can't produce bad fruit, and a bad tree cannot produce good fruit. ¹⁹ Every tree that produces bad fruit will be chopped down and burned. ²⁰ You can tell who the false prophets are by their deeds.

Here's a different TRUE and FALSE test. Jesus tells his followers how to discover which prophets or teachers are true or false.

You can tell by watching the things they do!

If their lives don't match their words – be careful about believing what they say.

Prayer: Thank you Jesus, you are the best teacher. Help me to learn from you and also from other good people and people who follow you.

Hong says he's the best goaler – but that's not what the scorecard shows.

Two kinds of people

The Hotshots know that just listening to the game plan won't win the match. They must obey the coach's instructions.

Matthew 7:24-27

[24] Anyone who hears and obeys these teachings of mine is like a wise person who built a house on solid rock. [25] Rain poured down, rivers flooded, and winds beat against that house. But it didn't fall, because it was built on solid rock.

[26] Anyone who hears my teachings and doesn't obey them is like a foolish person who built a house on sand. [27] The rain poured down, the rivers flooded, and the winds blew and beat against that house. Finally, it fell with a crash.

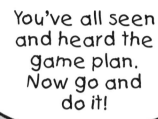

You've all seen and heard the game plan. Now go and do it!

This is a 'good news' and 'bad news' story.
Make two pictures on the next page, for this story.

continued overpage

The good news and the bad news

The Good News

Draw a picture of a house that is standing safely in a storm. When we hear and obey what Jesus teaches, we are

WISE / FOOLISH *(circle one)*

like this builder

The Bad News

Draw a picture of a house that is falling down in a storm. When we stop listening to what Jesus teaches, we are

WISE / FOOLISH *(circle one)*

like this builder.

Congratulations!

You have just read the main parts of the famous 'Sermon on the Mount'. What did you think of it? What do you think the people listening to it thought of it?

Now the next part of this Hotshots book will help us find out about how some followers of Jesus tried to do what Jesus taught.

First we will find out how Jesus showed his friends a good example.

The King who doesn't mind serving

3

Think of a job you don't like doing.

Jesus had something to teach his friends about such jobs

John 13:3-5

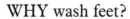

³ Jesus knew that he had come from God and would go back to God. He also knew that the Father had given him complete power. ⁴ So during the meal Jesus got up, removed his outer garment, and wrapped a towel around his waist. ⁵ He put some water into a large bowl. Then he began washing his disciples' feet and drying them with the towel he was wearing.

WHY wash feet?

The roads were dusty.
People wore sandals.

Every house had water pots
at the front door for the servants
to wash guests' feet.

WHO did it?

There were no servants at this house.
So who did the job?

During the meal, Jesus decided to teach
his disciples something important.

Prayer: *Lord Jesus, help me to be like you and do the thing no one else wants to do.*

Surprises for everyone

When someone you know does something unexpected you look at them quite differently, don't you?

John 13:6-10a

⁶ But when he came to Simon Peter, that disciple asked, "Lord, are you going to wash my feet?"

⁷ Jesus answered, "You don't really know what I am doing, but later you will understand."

⁸ "You'll never wash my feet!" Peter replied.

"If I don't wash you," Jesus told him, "you don't really belong to me."

⁹ Peter said, "Lord, don't wash just my feet. Wash my hands and my head."

¹⁰ Jesus answered, "People who have bathed and are clean all over need to wash just their feet.

What a surprise for the disciples!

Why was Jesus, their leader doing such a dirty job?

No important person they knew would wash smelly feet. Ugh!

"What was happening?" they wondered. Soon they would understand.

Draw the surprised looks on the disciples' faces.

Prayer: *Sometimes I find things about you hard to understand. Please help me dear God.*

25 Copying Jesus

Copying Jesus *continued ...*

Jeff invited the Hotshots to the 'Bullets' training session.

The Bullets were a good example to the Hotshots. Jesus showed a good example to his friends about caring for one another.

John 13:12-17

[12] After Jesus had washed his disciples' feet and had put his outer garment back on, he sat down again. Then he said:

"Do you understand what I have done? [13] You call me your teacher and Lord, and you should, because that is who I am. [14] And if your Lord and teacher has washed your feet, you should do the same for each other. [15] I have set the example, and you should do for each other exactly what I have done for you. [16] I tell you for certain that servants aren't greater than their master, and messengers aren't greater than the one who sent them. [17] You know these things, and God will bless you, if you do them."

Now the disciples understood.

Jesus had shown them that they must not be too proud to treat *everyone* in a loving and caring way.

Think and Pray:

How can I copy Jesus' example of loving and working to help others today?

26 Bartimaeus

In Jesus' time there were no pensions for disabled people, which is why they were forced to beg for money.

Mark 10:46-48

⁴⁶ Jesus and his disciples went to Jericho. And as they were leaving, they were followed by a large crowd. A blind beggar by the name of Bartimaeus son of Timaeus was sitting beside the road. ⁴⁷ When he heard that it was Jesus from Nazareth, he shouted, "Jesus, Son of David, have pity on me!" ⁴⁸ Many people told the man to stop, but he shouted even louder, "Son of David, have pity on me!"

Bartimaeus was determined to meet Jesus but some bossy people told him to be quiet. He was not put off. What did Bartimaeus do?

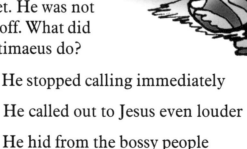

- [ ] He stopped calling immediately
- [ ] He called out to Jesus even louder
- [ ] He hid from the bossy people

Think and pray:
Do I ever let what others say put me off following Jesus?

I can see!

Close your eyes. Imagine what it would be like to have never seen a thing.

Mark 10:49-52

49 Jesus stopped and said, "Call him over!"

They called out to the blind man and said, "Don't be afraid! Come on! He is calling for you." 50 The man threw off his coat as he jumped up and ran to Jesus.

51 Jesus asked, "What do you want me to do for you?"

The blind man answered, "Master, I want to see!"

52 Jesus told him, "You may go. Your eyes are healed because of your faith."

Straight away the man could see, and he went down the road with Jesus.

Draw the changes in the **second** face when:

- **Bartimaeus believed Jesus could help him**
- **He asked Jesus to heal his eyes**
- **He was healed because of his faith in Jesus**

Prayer:

Thank you Jesus that you helped people in great need. Please care for

_____ *today.*

(Write someone's name who needs help from Jesus.)

Before
Master,
I want to see

After
Go, your eyes are healed because of your faith

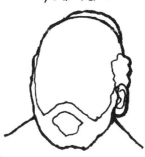

28 A boy and a picnic

4

The Hotshots have a problem. Where will they find enough money for new uniforms for the whole team?

John 6:5-9

[5] When Jesus saw the large crowd coming toward him, he asked Philip, "Where will we get enough food to feed all these people?" [6] He said this to test Philip, since he already knew what he was going to do.

[7] Philip answered, "Don't you know that it would take almost a year's wages just to buy only a little bread for each of these people?"

[8] Andrew, the brother of Simon Peter, was one of the disciples. He spoke up and said, [9] "There is a boy here who has five small loaves of barley bread and two fish. But what good is that with all these people?"

What seemed a big problem for Phillip and Andrew was not a problem for Jesus. He already knew what *he* would do. A young boy was part of his idea. Imagine how he felt when the disciple found him.

Prayer: *I'm glad that you can use me in you plans dear God, even though I'm only young.*

Let's sell chocolates.

A car wash is a good idea.

That wouldn't raise enough.

Food for everyone

Sometimes when you go out you think you will never get anything to eat. Then you are called to sit down and you've never seen so much beautiful food. This story is a bit like that.

John 6:10-15

[10] The ground was covered with grass, and Jesus told his disciples to get everyone to sit down. About 5000 thousand men were in the crowd. [11] Jesus took the bread in his hands and gave thanks to God. Then he passed the bread to the people, and he did the same with the fish, until everyone had plenty to eat.

[12] The people ate all they wanted, and Jesus told his disciples to gather up the leftovers, so that nothing would be wasted. [13] The disciples gathered them up and filled 12 large baskets with what was left over from the five barley loaves.

[14] After the people had seen Jesus work this miracle, they began saying, "This must be the Prophet who is to come into the world!" [15] Jesus realised that they would try to force him to be their king. So he went up on a mountain, where he could be alone.

What a wonderful thing to happen. It was made possible because a boy shared his lunch with Jesus. What an amazing happening! Imagine how the boy felt at the end.

Thought: Good things happen when we work together with God.

Do you like maths? Here's a very strange sum.

Miracle Maths

$$
\begin{aligned}
&\text{Jesus} \\
+\ &\text{1 Boy} \\
+\ &\text{5 Loaves} \\
+\ &\text{2 Fish} \\
\hline
=\ &\text{5000} \quad \text{with 12 remainder baskets}
\end{aligned}
$$

Some women who followed Jesus

Men and women, young people and old, are all welcome as Jesus' followers.

Luke 8:1-3

[1] Soon after this, Jesus was going through towns and villages, telling the good news about God's kingdom. His twelve apostles were with him, [2] and so were some women who had been healed of evil spirits and all sorts of diseases. One of the women was Mary Magdalene, who once had seven demons in her. [3] Joanna, Susanna, and many others had also used what they owned to help Jesus and his disciples. Joanna's husband Chuza was one of Herod's officials.

Having been helped by Jesus, these women also wanted to follow him.

What special thing did these and many other women do to help Jesus?

Fill in the missing words from verse 3.

They __ __ __ __ what they __ __ __ __ __

to help Jesus and his disciples.

Prayer:
Thank you God that all kinds of women and men are welcome in your family.

Unjumble the words to find the names of some women who followed Jesus

y m a r   **a n j o n a**   **u s n a s a n**

__ __ __ __   __ __ __ __ __ __   __ __ __ __ __ __ __

31   A mum who had the wrong idea

31   A mum who had the wrong idea

Long ago, to sit beside the King was a very special privilege. It showed you were a powerful and important person.

Matthew 20:20-23

20 The mother of James and John came to Jesus with her two sons. She knelt down and started begging him to do something for her. 21 Jesus asked her what she wanted, and she said, "When you come into your kingdom, please let one of my sons sit at your right side and the other at your left."

22 Jesus answered, "Not one of you knows what you are asking. Are you able to drink from the cup that I must soon drink from?"

James and John said, "Yes, we are!"

23 Jesus replied, "You certainly will drink from my cup! But it isn't for me to say who will sit at my right side and at my left. That is for my Father to say."

...and a special thank you to Kim, who puts away all the equipment correctly after each session, without being asked.

'Please let my sons be next to you in importance when your kingdom comes,' asked James and John's mother. This mother did not understand that God's Kingdom is *not* about being important, powerful or wealthy – it's about serving other people.

Think:
In an earlier story in this book, Jesus taught this fact to the disciples? Can you remember the story? Check your memory by checking readings 23,24,25 on pages 36-39.

32 Righting a wrong idea

Remember the mother of James and John?
Now she is confused and the other disciples are angry.

Jesus speaks clearly to put things right.

Matthew 20:24-28

24 When the ten other disciples heard this, they were angry with the two brothers. 25 But Jesus called the disciples together and said:

"You know that foreign rulers like to order their people around. And their great leaders have full power over everyone they rule. 26 But don't act like them. If you want to be great, you must be the servant of all the others. 27 And if you want to be first, you must be the slave of the rest. 28 The Son of Man did not come to be a slave master, but a slave who will give his life to rescue many people."

> If you want to be great, you must be the servant of all the others.

Very often the way God's kingdom works is the *opposite* of how people normally behave.

Righting a wrong idea
continued ...

The lists on the right describe two very different kingdoms. Decide which list talks about the way things should be in **God's Kingdom** and which list talks about **human kingdoms**. At the bottom of one list write 'How God wants us to be' and on the other write 'How people often are'.

Prayer: *Thank you Jesus for teaching us your way and inviting us into your Kingdom.*

_____ Kingdom

- kind
- serving others
- caring for everyone
- humble like a slave

_____ Kingdom

- powerful
- order others around
- want to be Number 1 in the land
- want to be great

How embarrassing!

Have you ever had weird dreams like going to school in your pyjamas? Or walking down the street and realising you had no clothes on?

Something embarrassing like that really happened to a young man on the sad day that Jesus was arrested. Read about it.

Mark 14:51-52

51 One of them was a young man who was wearing only a linen cloth. And when the men grabbed him, 52 he left the cloth behind and ran away naked.

This young man liked hanging around with Jesus and learning from him. But just now, if he stayed around he'd get into trouble. Imagine how he felt, this ordinary, scared, embarrassed young guy. But he'd rather be laughed at than go to jail. This same person, Mark, later wrote a book that millions of people still read today – Mark's gospel!

Prayer: *Dear God, thank you that you want all of us to be your friends, no matter how scared or silly we feel sometimes.*

Mark's News

Remember the young man who escaped from the trouble in the garden? He lost his clothes as he ran! Embarrassing!

Much later on he wrote the story of Jesus. We usually call this story 'The Gospel of Mark'.

MINI QUIZ

1. How many Gospels are there in the Bible? _____
   (Look in your Bible or ask a parent.)

2. What does the word 'Gospel' mean? *(Tick one)*
   ☐ Jesus the teacher   ☐ Good News   ☐ Church on Sunday

3. What are the names of all the Gospels?
   _____

4. Which Gospel writer also wrote the Book of Acts?
   _____

34 Mark finds a job

One week Kim played badly, making some stupid mistakes. She didn't want to show up to training the next week, but Jeff told her the team really needed her. Everyone plays badly sometimes.

Acts 12:25

25 And after Barnabas and Saul had done the work they were sent to do, they went back to Jerusalem with John, whose other name was Mark.

Acts 13:5

5 They arrived at Salamis and began to preach God's message in the Jewish meeting places. They also had John as a helper.

Prayer: *Dear God, thank you for understanding that we all have bad days and make mistakes. Thank you for loving us through our different moods.*

Mark, the guy who ran away naked, is now helping Saul. Saul, also called Paul, became one of the biggest heroes of the New Testament!
If you were Mark, after running away and leaving Jesus, how would you feel?

☐ Embarrassed?

☐ Ashamed?

☐ Wanting another chance?

Answers from page 49: 1. Four, 2. Good News, 3. Matthew, Mark, Luke John, 4. Luke

Gutsy Joseph

Chris told Jeff about an unpopular kid at school who was always left out. As a follower of Jesus Chris thought he should try and be friends with this kid, even if he might get teased for it and maybe even lose friends.

Mark 15:42-46

[42] It was now the evening before the Sabbath, and the Jewish people were getting ready for that sacred day. [43] A man named Joseph from Arimathea was brave enough to ask Pilate for the body of Jesus. Joseph was a highly respected member of the Jewish council, and he was also waiting for God's kingdom to come.

[44] Pilate was surprised to hear that Jesus was already dead, and he called in the army officer to find out if Jesus had been dead very long. [45] After the officer told him, Pilate let Joseph have Jesus' body.

[46] Joseph bought a linen cloth and took the body down from the cross. He had it wrapped in the cloth, and he put it in a tomb that had been cut into solid rock. Then he rolled a big stone against the entrance to the tomb.

continued overpage

Gutsy Joseph *continued ...*

Joseph was an important man who could get into trouble for asking to bury Jesus' body. But he was brave enough to do what he thought was right.

Prayer:
God, sometimes when we follow you we need to be brave. Help us at these times.

MINI QUIZ

Can you think of two other famous Josephs in the Bible?

1. (Look at Genesis chapter 37 in the Old Testament)

_____

_____

2. (Matthew chapter 1, verses 18-20 in the New Testament)

_____

_____

36 Three women hang in there

Emily rarely shoots the most goals but she never misses training. She thinks carefully about all that the coach Jeff tells them, and always plays her best.

Matthew 27:55-56

[55] Many women had come with Jesus from Galilee to be of help to him, and they were there, looking on from a distance. [56] Mary Magdalene, Mary the mother of James and Joseph, and the mother of James and John were some of these women.

Prayer: *Dear God, we can't always do exciting things. Sometimes we just have to be faithful and try to quietly follow in your way.*

A number of women followed Jesus. Even when things got tough, and lots of his other followers ran away, they were…

(Look on the ball to find the two letters missing at the beginning of each word)

__ __ AVE

__ __ ITHFUL

__ __ MBLE

__ __ VING

37 The big surprise

> I don't know what's wrong with Mum, I think Dad is worried about her.

Sometimes our worries turn out quite differently to what we feared might happen.

Mark 16:1-4

[1] After the Sabbath, Mary Magdalene, Salome, and Mary the mother of James bought some spices to put on Jesus' body. [2] Very early on Sunday morning, just as the sun was coming up, they went to the tomb. [3] On their way, they were asking one another, "Who will roll the stone away from the entrance for us?" [4] But when they looked, they saw that the stone had already been rolled away. And it was a huge stone!

> Hey, how cool! I'm going to be a big brother. Mum's having a baby.

How do you think the two Marys and Salome felt that morning?
(Tick the right boxes)

☐ Sad that Jesus had died?

☐ Caring enough to put spices on his body?

☐ Worried about how they would get into the tomb?

☐ Astonished that the HUGE stone was rolled away?

☐ Frightened, wondering what had happened?

☐ All of the above!

Prayer: *You are the God of surprises and new life. Help us to welcome your wonderful surprises.*

How good is this news?

Don't be afraid! Jesus is alive!

Mark 16:5-7

5 The women went into the tomb, and on the right side they saw a young man in a white robe sitting there. They were alarmed.

6 The man said, "Don't be alarmed! You are looking for Jesus from Nazareth, who was nailed to a cross. God has raised him to life, and he isn't here. You can see the place where they put his body. 7 Now go and tell his disciples, and especially Peter, that he will go ahead of you to Galilee. You will see him there, just as he told you."

Some things seem unbelievable.

It probably took a few seconds for Dan to believe the news that his mother was really OK. She was feeling unwell because she was having a baby, not because she was seriously ill! It is hard for people to believe that God raised Jesus to life but Christians believe that Jesus' death was not the end of him even though we don't understand how. Jesus is still around today, alive, and able to be close to us.

Swap the first and last letters of each word to decode the message:

TOND EB DFRAIA!   SESUJ SI ELIVA!

Prayer: Thank you God that Jesus didn't just die and disappear. Thank you that because of his new life, we can experience you in our lives.

39 Share the news!

How about bringing a friend along next week to play and hear about God's good news.

Last Friday, Jeff talked to the Hotshots about sharing what they knew about Jesus with other kids.

Matthew 28:8-10

8 The women were frightened and yet very happy, as they hurried from the tomb and ran to tell his disciples. 9 Suddenly Jesus met them and greeted them. They went near him, held on to his feet, and worshipped him. 10 Then Jesus said, "Don't be afraid! Tell my followers to go to Galilee. They will see me there."

People might think they were crazy, but the women knew they had to share their amazing and wonderful news.

Prayer: Dear God, help us to be brave. Help us to share the good news that you care for us and want to be part of our lives.

DECODE: divide this long word in the right places to make a sentence:

JESUSISALIVEANDFILLSUSWITHJOYANDCOURAGE

40 Too good to be true

Luke 24:9-12

9-10 Mary Magdalene, Joanna, Mary the mother of James, and some other women were the ones who had gone to the tomb. When they returned, they told the eleven apostles and the others what had happened. 11 The apostles thought it was all nonsense, and they wouldn't believe.

12 But Peter ran to the tomb. And when he stooped down and looked in, he saw only the burial clothes. Then he returned, wondering what had happened.

Those poor women! No one believed them! Everyone thought they were crazy! Peter went to investigate, but he didn't understand what had happened and came back wondering.

Imagine you are Peter. What might be going through your mind?

- ☐ I don't believe it!
- ☐ They're dreaming
- ☐ I wish they were right, but it's impossible
- ☐ Maybe … can I dare to hope?

Prayer idea:
Think about some unexpected, wonderful things that have happened in your life. Then think about some of the ways that God seems to be alive and working in the world. Continue to look out for these things and thank God for them.

Peter dives in the deep end

Anna is an 'over-the-top' kid. When the Hotshots win a game, score a goal, or she plays well at training, Anna goes jumping, even cartwheeling all over the place. 'She's embarrassing,' the other kids say, but Jeff loves her enthusiasm.

John 21:1-7

[1] Jesus later appeared to his disciples along the shore of Lake Tiberias. [2] Simon Peter, Thomas the Twin, Nathanael from Cana in Galilee, and the brothers James and John, were there, together with two other disciples. [3] Simon Peter said, "I'm going fishing!"

The others said, "We'll go with you." They went out in their boat. But they didn't catch a thing that night.

[4] Early the next morning Jesus stood on the shore, but the disciples did not realise who he was. [5] Jesus shouted, "Friends, have you caught anything?"

"No!" they answered.

[6] So he told them, "Let your net down on the right side of your boat, and you will catch some fish." They did, and the net was so full of fish that they couldn't drag it up into the boat.

[7] Jesus' favourite disciple told Peter, "It's the Lord!" When Simon heard that it was the Lord, he put on the clothes that he had taken off while he was working. Then he jumped into the water.

Peter dives in the deep end *continued ...*

Peter's reactions were always over-the-top. He even tried to walk on top of water once to get to Jesus! (If you're interested, you can find this story in Matthew 14:22-33).

Here he is again, jumping straight into the lake fully clothed, because he was so excited to see the risen Jesus.

Prayer: *Thank you, God, for the times when I'm full of energy and enthusiasm.*

The big catch

[7] Jesus' favourite disciple told Peter, "It's the Lord!" When Simon heard that it was the Lord, he put on the clothes that he had taken off while he was working. Then he jumped in the water. [8] The boat was only about 100 metres from shore. So the other disciples stayed in the boat and dragged in the net full of fish.

[9] When the disciples got out of the boat, they saw some bread and a charcoal fire with fish on it. [10] Jesus told his disciples, "Bring some of the fish you just caught." [11] Simon Peter got back into the boat and dragged the net to shore. In it were 153 large fish, but still the net didn't rip.

Jesus did lots of miracles. Usually they were healing miracles. He even raised people from the dead. And this is pretty hard for us to understand.

Here is another miracle, or at least something very unusual. This story helps us to understand that Jesus made the ordinary lives of his followers full: full of challenge, excitement, struggle, joy, companionship and faith.

The big catch
continued ...

In another story, Jesus told his disciples that they would go fishing for people! By this he meant that through his followers, many people would learn about Jesus and become followers themselves.

Write: Who is the person who most helps you to be a follower of Jesus? Write the person's name here

_____

Prayer: *Thanks God for the way you fill our lives with challenge. Give us companions as we try to follow your way. Thank you.*

Draw here a story you have heard or read of Jesus doing amazing things.

Fish 'n' chips on the beach

Sometimes the Hotshots have fish and chips together on a Friday night after training. They love it. Sharing food together is always special.

John 21:12-14

¹² Jesus said, "Come and eat!" But none of the disciples dared ask who he was. They knew he was the Lord. ¹³ Jesus took the bread in his hands and gave some of it to his disciples. He did the same with the fish. ¹⁴ This was the third time that Jesus appeared to his disciples after he was raised from death.

Prayer: *Thank you God for the food we have every day. Help us to share what we have and our friendship with others.*

Well not quite fish and chips, but fish and bread anyway. Jesus loved sharing food with people. He often got into trouble because he liked to eat with people who were a bit scruffy. And here again, Jesus is giving his friends food. In another story, two of Jesus followers only recognised him when they noticed how he broke the bread (if you're interested see Luke 24:13-33).

Can you de-code this sentence?

Code: a=1, e=2, i=3, u=5

J2S5S G1V2 H3S D3SC3PL2S BR21D 1ND F3SH

_ _ _ _ _   _ _ _ _   _ _ _   _ _ _ _ _ _ _

_ _ _ _ _   _ _ _   _ _ _ _

More about Peter

Chris has a temper. He gets angry on the court, does stupid things and keeps getting fouled off. Jeff takes this seriously, taking Chris off then talking to him later. But next game, he gives him another chance.

Next time he elbows me, I'll give it to him!

John 21:15,17-19

[15] When Jesus and his disciples had finished eating, he asked, "Simon son of John, do you love me more than the others do?"

Simon Peter answered, "Yes, Lord, you know I do!"

"Then feed my lambs," Jesus said.

[17] Jesus asked a third time, "Simon son of John, do you love me?" Peter was hurt because Jesus had asked him three times if he loved him. So he told Jesus, "Lord, you know everything. You know I love you."

Jesus replied, "Feed my sheep. [18] I tell you for certain that when you were a young man, you dressed yourself and went wherever you wanted to go. But when you are old, you will hold out your hands. Then others will wrap your belt around you and lead you where you don't want to go."

[19] Jesus said this to tell how Peter would die and bring honour to God. Then he said to Peter, "Follow me!"

We've read before about Peter's enthusiasm and some of the really stupid things he does. Earlier in the story, Peter let Jesus down badly (Luke 22:54-62). Jesus wasn't about to say this didn't matter. It mattered heaps. But Jesus forgave Peter, and then gave him a job to do.

continued overpage

More about Peter *continued ...*

When Jesus talked to Peter
he said: *(Tick the right one)*

☐ Hey Peter, it doesn't
matter, let's just forget it

☐ I'll never speak to you
again because you let
me down

☐ What you did was wrong,
but I forgive you and
I have things for you to do

Prayer: *God, forgive us when we
do things that hurt others
or ourselves. Thank you
that you always give us
another chance. Thank you
that, like a good parent,
you never stop loving us.*

45 Thomas refuses to be sucked in

Hong takes a bit of convincing. If the others tell him something good (like Jeff has got them all free tickets to a really top basketball match), he just says, 'oh yeah, right'.

That's just too good to be true.

John 20:24-25

24 Although Thomas the Twin was one of the twelve disciples, he wasn't with the others when Jesus appeared to them. 25 So they told him, "We have seen the Lord!"

But Thomas said, "First, I must see the nail scars in his hands and touch them with my finger. I must put my hand where the spear went into his side. I won't believe unless I do this!"

Prayer: *God, we don't want to be easily sucked in. But open our eyes to the many wonderful things that happen in our lives, and the unexpected places we might find you.*

Thomas couldn't believe that Jesus was alive again. No way! Not until he'd seen Jesus with his own eyes, and touched him with his own hands.

Tick what you think is the right box:

Do you think it's good to be:

☐ Never sucked in, always doubtful

☐ Believing everything anyone tells you

☐ Not an idiot, but open to the wonderful surprises in life

46   Seeing is believing

It's really you Lord!

Have you ever said, 'Pull the other leg', then found out the thing was true. That's how Thomas felt. Read on.

John 20:26-29

²⁶ A week later the disciples were together again. This time, Thomas was with them. Jesus came in while the doors were still locked and stood in the middle of the group. He greeted his disciples ²⁷ and said to Thomas, "Put your finger here and look at my hands! Put your hand into my side. Stop doubting and have faith!"

²⁸ Thomas replied, "You are my Lord and my God!"

²⁹ Jesus said, "Thomas, do you have faith because you have seen me? The people who have faith in me without seeing me are the ones who are really blessed!"

Well, Jesus certainly took Thomas seriously. He even let him touch the deep wound in his side. And Thomas believed all right.

Then Jesus went on to say that the people who are really blessed are the ones who believe without seeing and touching. Could this be us?

CODE: Cross out the first and last letters of each word to get the meaning of this sentence:

TBLESSEDW BAREL CTHOSED TWHOT UDOT INOTE ISEEK CANDL ESTILLM ABELIEVEO

Prayer: *God, sometimes it's hard to know what to believe. Help us to think and question, but also to listen to what the Bible, other Christians and our own hearts tell us about you.*

47

There's more to life than money

One Friday night, the Hotshots and Jeff were having fish and chips together. The team kept talking about serious stuff. Anna told the gang about her Uncle and Auntie, how incredibly rich they were. What seemed most important to them was money and things: big house, cars, swimming pool, clothes.

Jeff said, 'There are lots of people like that in our society. And not only rich people, either. But Jesus said that some things in life are much more important than money."

They have everything anyone could possibly want, but they don't seem very happy.

continued overpage

There's more to life than money *continued ...*

Matthew 19:16-22

¹⁶ A man came to Jesus and asked, "Teacher, what good thing must I do to have eternal life?"

¹⁷ Jesus said to him, "Why do you ask me about what is good? Only God is good. If you want to have eternal life, you must obey his commandments."

¹⁸ Which ones?" the man asked.

Jesus answered, "Do not murder. Be faithful in marriage. Do not steal. Do not tell lies about others. ¹⁹ Respect your father and mother. And love others as much as you love yourself." ²⁰ The young man said, "I've obeyed all of these. What else must I do?"

²¹ Jesus replied, "If you want to be perfect, go sell everything you own! Give the money to the poor, and you will have riches in heaven. Then come and be my follower." ²² When the young man heard this, he was sad, because he was very rich.

TICK THE BOXES

What are the things in life that are most important to you?

(Hint: there are no right or wrong answers here!)

☐ sport   ☐ books

☐ friends   ☐ music

☐ computer games   ☐ food

☐ family   ☐ clothes

☐ animals   ☐ _____

Prayer: *God, we live in a society where money and the things it can buy are seen as very important. Help us to be brave enough to see things differently.*

48 The camel and the needle

48

After their talk about money, Jeff told the Hotshots this story of Jesus.

Matthew 19:23-24

23 Jesus said to his disciples, "It's terribly hard for rich people to get into the kingdom of heaven! 24 In fact, it's easier for a camel to go through the eye of a needle than for a rich person to get into God's kingdom."

See if you can draw a really weird picture: a camel going through the eye of a needle.

continued overpage

The camel and the needle *continued ...*

Jesus certainly had some funny stories.
You have to think hard about this one.
It is not easy to understand.

What do you think Jesus meant in this story?
Tick a box:

- ☐ God hates rich people
- ☐ Rich people are always bad, poor people are always good
- ☐ It's hard to get close to God when you like money and things too much
- ☐ It's hard to get close to God when you are too worried about money and things
- ☐ Sometimes we get closest to God when we are feeling weak and down
- ☐ When we have too much stuff, it's easy to forget that we depend on God for everything

Which boxes did you tick? This is a difficult story, but I ticked the last four. Think about it.

Prayer:
Dear God, thank you that we have food and shelter. Help us never to forget that all good things come from you. Help us to remember that many children in the world aren't so lucky.

Acts – a funny name for a book

1. The book of Acts is a bit different from other books in the New Testament. It's in between what we call the Gospels and the Epistles. Many people skip past it without realising there are some great stories there.

2. The Gospels tell the story of Jesus' life on earth.

3. 'Epistles' is an old fashioned way of saying letters, and that's what the Epistles are: letters from Paul, Peter, John and other church leaders to followers of Jesus in other places. The letters were written to encourage and sometimes correct these followers. And in between the Gospels and the Epistles comes Acts, a book all on its own.

continued overpage

4. 'Acts' is a short way of saying 'The Acts of the Apostles', just as we say 'Luke' rather than say 'The Gospel according to Saint Luke'. Luke wrote both books.

5. Acts is the sequel to Luke. You may have seen sequels at the movies. They tell the next part of the story. The 'Star Wars' stories are like that, and 'Babe', 'Star Trek', and many others.

6. The Acts, of course, means the things people do. Who do? The Apostles. And who are they? They were the first followers of Jesus. Acts tells the story of what happened to the earliest Christians who started following Jesus soon after he came alive again and left the earth.

7. Here is where you find what they learnt about Jesus, the trouble they got into, the good things they did.

8. Some of them were put in prison or even killed because of their love for Jesus. It was tough being a Christian in those days. (In some countries it still is very hard to live as a follower of Jesus.)

9. One of the main characters in Acts is Paul, who spread the good news of Jesus over many parts of the world.

10. In Acts, we read that people often argued about who could be a Christian: who was in and who was out. The very best news in Acts is that no one is out. God loves and welcomes everyone, and wants everyone to follow God and be God's friend.

49   Helping other people

Acts 9:36-38

36 In Joppa there was a follower named Tabitha. Her Greek name was Dorcas, which means "deer." She was always doing good things for people and had given much to the poor. 37 But she got sick and died, and her body was washed and placed in an upstairs room. 38 Joppa wasn't far from Lydda, and the followers heard that Peter was there. They sent two men to say to him, "Please come with us as quickly as you can!"

Prayer: *Thank you God that we have enough money. Help us to be generous to others.*

One way of making sure that money isn't too important in your life is to give it away!

We donate to Community Aid Abroad every year.

I know my Mum and Dad give money to the church every week.

Followers of Jesus have always tried to assist people who need help. Very early Christians like Dorcas helped set an example for other Christians to follow.

If you would like to give some of your pocket money to a worthy cause, talk about it with your parents. Together find out the names of two particular helping organisations you might wish to support and send off for their literature.

Not just money

Giving money isn't the only way to help others.
In today's story, we learn how Dorcas helped others.

Acts 9:39

[39] Straight away, Peter went with them.

The men took Peter upstairs into the room. Many widows were there crying. They showed him the coats and clothes that Dorcas had made while she was still alive.

Dorcas made clothes for widows and their children. In those days, widows were usually very poor and many people looked down on them. Not Dorcas. Like Jesus, she didn't care whether the people she mixed with were popular or rich. If people needed her, she would help.

Can you think of ways you could help others, for example visiting someone lonely? Write your ideas on the note page above.

Prayer: Thank you for all the people who have helped us during our lives. Show us ways of helping others.

51 Dorcas alive again

The Hotshots were playing the best team in the league. They couldn't possibly win, but somehow they did. Working together as a team, they played better than they believed possible.

Acts 9:40-43

[40] After Peter had sent everyone out of the room, he knelt down and prayed. Then he turned to the body of Dorcas and said, "Tabitha, get up!" The woman opened her eyes, and when she saw Peter, she sat up. [41] He took her by the hand and helped her to her feet.

Peter called in the widows and the other followers and showed them that Dorcas had been raised from death. [42] Everyone in Joppa heard what had happened, and many of them put their faith in the Lord. [43] Peter stayed on for a while in Joppa in the house of a man named Simon, who made leather.

Dorcas alive again *continued ...*

At school, Kim had been fighting with another kid for weeks. She thought it would never end. But it did. This other kid had done something really mean to her and Kim thought she'd never forgive her. But after thinking and praying about it, Kim decided she could forgive her.

A huge weight seemed to fall off her shoulders.

This miracle story is exciting to read but hard for us to imagine. We know Jesus raised people from the dead, and today's story tells us that sometimes his disciples did amazing things like this too.

If we are God's friends, we are able to do things we never thought possible, good things. Maybe not raising dead people. Maybe not even winning basketball matches, but things like forgiving people and changing our lives.

Prayer: *God, help us to expect you to make changes in our lives. Help us to look out for ways in which you are working in the world and in people we know.*

It takes all sorts

One day the Hotshots started talking about how different they were from one another. For a start, there were kids from four different races. Not bad for seven kids! Some of the things they noticed were that kids from the same ethnic group looked different from each other, had different sized families, hobbies and abilities on the basketball court. In fact, the Hotshots *are* different in just about every way. You could say they are unique...special and different.

Acts 16:12-14

[12] From there we went to Philippi, which is a Roman colony in the first district of Macedonia.

We spent several days in Philippi. [13] Then on the Sabbath we went outside the city gate to a place by the river, where we thought there would be a Jewish meeting place for prayer. We sat down and talked with the women who came. [14] One of them was Lydia, who was from the city of Thyatira and sold expensive purple cloth. She was a worshipper of the Lord God, and he made her willing to accept what Paul was saying.

It takes all sorts *continued* ...

Many of the followers of Jesus were women.
Here is another one: Lydia, who had an interesting and unusual job!

The people who followed God in the Old Testament and Jesus in the New Testament were all different too. God loves variety.

DE-CODE: Swap the first and last letter of each word to decode the message:

DOG EADM SU LLA TIFFEREND.
DOG SIKEL SU THAT YAW.

_____

_____

Prayer: *Thank you that we are all different and special.*
Thank you that you made us like this and love us just as we are.

53 Having people over

Acts 16:15,40

¹⁵ Then after she and her family were baptised, she kept on begging us, "If you think I really do have faith in the Lord, come stay in my home." Finally, we accepted her invitation.

⁴⁰ But Paul and Silas went straight to the home of Lydia, where they saw the Lord's followers and encouraged them. Then they left.

I love visiting cousins and friends. We have great food.

And I can think of one kid at school who'd love to be asked back to my house.

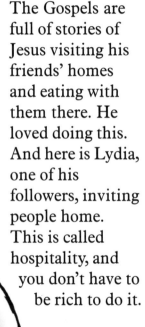

The Gospels are full of stories of Jesus visiting his friends' homes and eating with them there. He loved doing this. And here is Lydia, one of his followers, inviting people home. This is called hospitality, and you don't have to be rich to do it.

Having people over *continued ...*

TRUE OR FALSE QUIZ

To be hospitable you need:

Circle right answer

To have lots of money	True / False
To have a big house	True / False
To have a swimming pool	True / False
To be a fantastic cook	True / False
To be friendly and willing to share what you have	True / False

(Answers at the bottom of page 83)

Prayer: *Thanks, God, for all the people who have shared their lives and homes and hearts with us. Help us to see ways we can do this for others.*

These books will help you to understand the Bible. Make sure you get the whole set!

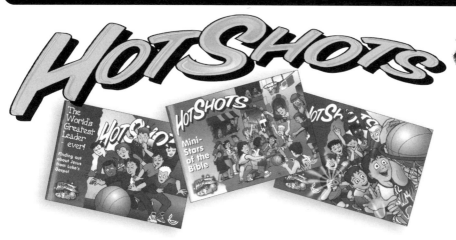

There are four books in the first *Hotshots* series. The whole Hotshots gang (that famous Little League Basketball team) is learning about the Bible. You can buy all four books from your nearest Scripture Union office or Christian bookshop.

- ◆ The World's Greatest Leader—ever!
- ◆ Mini-stars of the Bible
- ◆ Growing as a follower of Jesus
- ◆ Sticking Close to God

Then there is a second series—also called *Hotshots*. This features a different gang. They also meet every week in a kids club, but they have a secret. Shhh! They have their very own Time-ship, right in the very same place as their club house. And they have great Time Adventures. You can join with them.

Snapshots

If you feel that you're growing too old for *Hotshots*, you can join the *Snapshots* team. Designed for 9 and 10 year olds, *Snapshots* has a Bible reading for every day, with puzzles and activities. Ask Scripture Union how you can subscribe.

Paul and Silas in trouble

Acts 16:16-24

¹⁶ One day on our way to the place of prayer, we were met by a slave girl. She had a spirit in her that gave her the power to tell the future. By doing this she made a lot of money for her owners. ¹⁷ The girl followed Paul and the rest of us and kept yelling, "These men are servants of the Most High God! They are telling you how to be saved."

¹⁸ This went on for several days. Finally, Paul got so upset that he turned and said to the spirit, "In the name of Jesus Christ, I order you to leave this girl alone!" At once the evil spirit left her.

¹⁹ When the girl's owners realised that they had lost all chances for making more money, they grabbed Paul and Silas and dragged them into court. ²⁰ They told the officials, "These Jews are upsetting our city! ²¹ They are telling us to do things we Romans are not allowed to do."

²² The crowd joined in the attack on Paul and Silas. Then the officials tore the clothes off the two men and ordered them to be beaten with a whip. ²³ After they had been badly beaten, they were put in jail, and the jailer was told to guard them carefully. ²⁴ The jailer did as he was told. He put them deep inside the jail and chained their feet to heavy blocks of wood.

continued overpage

Paul and Silas in trouble
continued ...

People get very upset when they lose their chance to make plenty of money! When Paul and Silas set the slave girl free, her owners didn't appreciate it. They were now in big trouble for doing what they thought was right. Has this ever happened to you?

Can you think of a good thing to do which might land you in trouble?

Once a friend asked if I'd help him cheat in a test. I said no, and now he won't speak to me. Some of the other kids call me awful names.

_____

_____

_____

Prayer: *God, sometimes it's really hard to do what we think is right. Help us to be brave when this happens.*

Singing in prison

Have you ever visited a prison, or toured through an old one no longer in use as a prison?

Acts 16:25-26

[25] About midnight Paul and Silas were praying and singing praises to God, while the other prisoners listened. [26] Suddenly a strong earthquake shook the jail to its foundations. The doors opened, and the chains fell from all the prisoners.

continued overpage

Singing in prison *continued ...*

Did I tell you about my older sister? She was protesting against a uranium mine and ended up in jail for a night.

She said she felt good deep inside because she thought that she was doing the right thing ... I don't know if she was singing songs though!

All over the world, lots of people go to prison. Some have done nothing wrong – the people in power put them in prison because they didn't like what they believed. Amnesty International tries to help these prisoners.

Ask your parents or another adult, what they know about Amnesty or if they know any others who are in jail for what they believe.

Prayer: *Dear God, thank you for our freedom. Be with all people in prison, no matter the reason they are there.*

56 Beginning with Jesus

Acts 16:31

31 They replied, "Have faith in the Lord Jesus and you will be saved! This is also true for everyone who lives in your home."

Mark lines in the right places to make sense out of this line of letters:

HAVEFAITHINTHELORDJESUSANDYOUWILLBESAVED

Go to church and ask the people there if God has made a difference in their lives.

What an exciting way to start your life with Jesus! People begin following Jesus in different ways – some exciting, some quiet and ordinary. Some have lots of questions they don't understand.

If you would like to think about beginning as a follower of Jesus, turn to page 95 for help.

Prayer: Dear God, help us to find people who can teach us what it means to have faith in you.

Following and helping

Acts 16:32-34

³² Then Paul and Silas told him and everyone else in his house about the Lord. ³³ While it was still night, the jailer took them to a place where he could wash their cuts and bruises. Then he and everyone in his home were baptised. ³⁴ They were very glad that they had put their faith in God. After this, the jailer took Paul and Silas to his home and gave them something to eat.

This jailer is a practical man. He has just begun to follow Jesus and makes sure that Paul and Silas get their wounds washed and bandaged and have a good feed.

Anna tells her team-mates that in her church lots of people do practical things to care for others. They make casseroles, mow lawns, visit those who are sick and do lots of other stuff as well. That's important too.

Write down one practical thing you could do to help someone.

I know – I could walk the dog for the old lady next door. She's sick right now.

_____

Prayer: God, help me to notice ways to help someone else.

New life

Acts 20:7-12

7 On the first day of the week we met to break bread together. Paul spoke to the people until midnight because he was leaving the next morning. 8 In the upstairs room where we were meeting, there were a lot of lamps. 9 A young man by the name of Eutychus was sitting on a window sill. While Paul was speaking, the young man got very sleepy. Finally he went to sleep and fell three floors all the way down to the ground. When they picked him up, he was dead.

10 Paul went down and bent over Eutychus. He took him in his arms and said, "Don't worry! He's alive." 11 After Paul had gone back upstairs, he broke bread, and ate with us. He then spoke until dawn and left. 12 Then the followers took the young man home alive and were very happy.

Maybe it was a boring talk or the room was very hot. (Perhaps you feel like sleeping in church?!?)

But then another miracle happened!

continued overpage

New life *continued ...*

Talking of a new start, there is more about this on page 95.

Talking of a new start, there is more about this on page 95.

What do you think of this story?
(Tick a box—any box, there's no right answer)

☐ Unbelievable

☐ Maybe things like that happened back then

☐ Well, some pretty amazing things happen these days too

☐ Weird, but maybe we can learn something from it anyway

Eutychus was lucky. He had a whole new start in his life. God's love made the difference!

Prayer: *God, help us to be open to the new life that you want to give us.*

59 Good wishes

Acts 20:17, 22-24, 32-35

17 From Miletus, Paul sent a message for the church leaders at Ephesus to come and meet with him. 22 'I don't know what will happen to me in Jerusalem, but I must obey God's Spirit and go there. 23 In every city I visit, I am told by the Holy Spirit that I will be put in jail and will be in trouble in Jerusalem. 24 But I don't care what happens to me, as long as I finish the work that the Lord Jesus gave me to do. And that work is to tell the good news about God's great kindness…

32 I now place you in God's care. Remember the message about his great kindness! This message can help you and give you what belongs to you as God's people. 33 I have never wanted anyone's money or clothes. 34 You know how I have worked with my own hands to make a living for myself and my friends. 35 By everything I did, I showed how you should work to help everyone who is weak. Remember that our Lord Jesus said, "More blessings come from giving than from receiving".'

Was Paul brave or just stupid? He didn't care what happened to him, as long as he was able to spread the word about God's great kindness. He must have felt it was pretty important! Maybe if we understand how much God loves us and wants to give us good things, we will feel like giving to others too.

It does feel good to give

Yeah, I love Christmas because you have fun both getting and giving.

Look again at the wise words in verse 35. Choose your favourite coloured pen to underline them. Then write it neatly on a piece of card. Keep it as a bookmark or hang it as a sign in your room.

Prayer: *Dear God, thank you for the fun of getting and the pleasure of giving. Thank you for being such a great giving God.*

Goodbye Paul

Emily's Granny died last year. She remembers how sad it was seeing her for the last time when she was so sick. The other day, Emily's family went to visit Granny's grave and Emily felt a bit sad all over again. But also happy, because her Granny gave her so much love. She was such an important person in Emily's life.

What people important to you have died or moved away? If you can think of any, list their names:

_____

_____

_____

Acts 20:36-38

36 After Paul had finished speaking, he knelt down with all of them and prayed. 37 Everyone cried and hugged and kissed him. 38 They were especially sad because Paul had told them, "You will never see me again."

Then they went with him to the ship.

Goodbye Paul *continued ...*

Think about each person for a minute. Let yourself feel sad because they're not here any more, and also glad because you knew them.

Prayer: *Dear God, thank you for all the people who come into our lives*

Joining the followers of Jesus

The Hotshots have been discovering things about lots of people who became followers of Jesus. Do you remember Bartimaeus the blind man, John Mark the writer of the Gospel and Dorcas who made clothes for poor people? They were like a big family of friends. People can join that family today—even though it's nearly 2000 years later. That's why people often call this family, 'God's Forever Family'.

I follow Jesus because he loves me. Because I love him I want to serve him the very best way I can.

And there are many other reasons for becoming a follower of Jesus.

I follow Jesus because he died to save us and forgive us.

I follow Jesus because he's my friend and he's always there.

How to begin following Jesus

The first steps

Deciding whether to follow Jesus is like deciding which gate to use or which road to follow. Look at Jesus' words on page 30.

Jesus invites **everyone** to be his friends and followers. Some people say yes, but others don't accept.

Step One

Thank you

Say thank you to God for loving you and for promising to forgive you. Say thanks also for Jesus who came to show us the way and how to get rid of our sin.

Step Two

Sorry

Tell God you are sorry for the sin and wrong in your life. Ask for the forgiveness you need.

Step Three

Please

Ask God to live in your life and give you a new beginning. Ask also for help to obey. Say a prayer like this in your own words. Write it on a piece of paper.

If you really mean what you say, you can be sure God hears you and that you're now part of Jesus' family.

Write the date you prayed this prayer:

_____

CERTIFICATE

Scripture Union
and
The Hotshots Team

This is to certify that

. . . .

[write your name neatly]

has completed the stories and projects from
Hotshots – Growing as a Follower of Jesus

Signed: ....*Jeff*............................... Jeff   (Hotshots Coach)

Countersigned: .... (Parent or other adult)

Date: ....